POETIC MATURATION

"A Growth within Words"

WRITTEN BY: DANIEL D. TUCKER

For more poetry and updates visit

Instagram: @akingspoetry

Contents

Thanks

Introduction

In life, growth is inevitable. We must understand the importance of growing and evolving through life as we become older and hopefully much wiser. It is up to us to utilize the knowledge we gain along the way to place our minds and spirits in the best place.

Poetic Maturation is not just a book of poetry, it is a small map of my journey as a writer and as a man. I wanted to give all of me within this work. I wanted to share with you the journey of my life and craft thus far.

The reason I chose to name the book *Poetic Maturation "A Growth within Words"* is because I feel I have come so far as an artist and as a man. And in both of these areas I still have far to go. I decided to fill this book with a collection of poems that span from the beginning of my artistic journey up until the present day. As you read, you will see changes, in subject matter, language and the overall energy of my works. My views of love, religion, spirituality, and the world as a whole have changed throughout this time, and I wanted to be completely open and vulnerable with you in my art. Because that is what an artist is supposed to do. The young man I was in the past has not gone away, but rather he has begun to truly blossom.

One of the most important things to me in this world is my African heritage. I love my ancestry and I love my culture. I love my skin and I love my people. I hope that this book and all those to come will inspire all those that are able to read it.

I thank you for taking to time to come into my world. And I hope you enjoy your time inside my artistic realm.

<u>Dedication</u>

I dedicate this book and the creative energy that it entails, to the life and memory of my late brother Benjamin Keith Tucker Jr. May you always watch over me.

July 14th, 1983-July 2nd, 2010

Tell Me

If art is life

Then tell me

What death is

Would death be

All the great poems that

Nikki never finished

Or the steps Alvin choreographed

Which never touched a stage

Is it all the songs that

Billy never sang

Or could it be the *strange fruits*

Those southern trees would hang

If art is life

Then tell me what death is

Is it all the books

Never written

During Harlem's Renaissance

The unheard dreams

Of aspiring black teens

That wished to be like

Miles

Duke

And Coltrane

Is it all the films

Dorothy never starred in

The fights Jack didn't win

The novels Zora never wrote

The races Jesse didn't run

The Music Joplin never composed

If so

Then now I know

If art is life

Then death

Is not making it

Our Introduction
June 29th, 1985
I am introduced to you
And you to I

My eyes barely open
Blinded by the light
Yet finding safety
In the arms of the Woman
Who gave me life

We were two
As one
For nine months
Sharing a bond
That was by god
Touched

The shelter in which you gave
Is one that
Could never be manmade

And you placed
No blame upon
The absence
Of the man
From which part of me came

Your sacrifices guide my eyes
When times are light-less

Showing me

That my debt to you
Is forever priceless

Discipline was never missin'
In the recipe
Of my childhood
Therefore I stood
Strong

Because of you

Your punishment
Was a rare form of
Nourishment
Which fueled me with
The right amount of encouragement

And for that...I THANK YOU

A Queen

By the stars I could have sworn

Our hearts would align as one

And as sure as the Pyramids of Giza stand tall

I would have given my soul

To be the one she called *Her King*

The one her Essence mirrored with

The one her spirit found shelter in...

In that lifetime...

I would have surrendered *My Kingdom*

Just to share her presence

That was the Power...

Of her *ESSENCE*

African Iris

She is most precious

She is the very essence
Of a people strengthened through struggle

She is beauty unmatched
And a power
Untamed

She is the flame
That provides warmth
Upon the chilled sands
Of resting Pharaoh's

She is the rock
Of all Man

Kind
Strong
Loving
Humble
Caring

An African Queen
Who dares to be Daring

She is a flower

That rises in the sun

Surrounded by blades of grass
That grow only to adore
Her petals

To watch her gracefulness
In the midst of the wind

She is an inspiration
For her children

She is the Creator of life
The very maker of light

The soul of her people

And perhaps
The secret to life

She is

The "African Iris"

Our Forever's

Are marked

By the memories

Painted upon the walls

Of our minds

They create murals of

Love

Life

Friends

And the tragedies that have

Shaped our very foundation

Each day begins

With a footstep

Toward our envisioned destiny

And ends

With the realization of

Greatness in the makin'

Change

To all those who KNEW ME
Where have I gone?
Am I not the same man
That I was before?
Where is the old me?
That you say is not here
Have I truly left
Or is it you who's disappeared?

Children of the 'Pool Players' (Homage to Gwendolyn Brooks)

I'm so fly. I
Get high. I

Steal wheels. I
Just chill. I

Sip liq. I
Quit quick. I

Watched you. I
Died too.

Temptation

Birthed form a *deep conversation*

I long for *the introduction* of *our lips*

Thoughts of the *deepest sensation*

Creating the most *sensual formation* of two nations

Connected by the slightest *penetration*

I'm *captivated* by every part of *you*

From the *lips* upon your *face*

To the *hips* below your *waist*

By the *coloring* of your *eyes*

To the *thundering* of your *thighs*

At times I *wonder*

Tis it a must that I *lust* for your heavenly *touch*

Wanting to *know* your every *in* and *out*

As I *hold* you while going *in* and out your most *sensitive region*

But I know these *thoughts* within my *mind* can never become *physical actions*

It is a mere *lustful attraction*

Which will only bring the *slightest* bit of *satisfaction*

Therefore I *relax* and...

Act as if *nothing* ever happened

Because I know I must *resist* this *devilish sensation.*

Which we call.....*TEMPTATION*

I

Write because of *Maya*
Stand because of *Malcom*
March because of *Martin*
Learn because of *Frederick*
Believe because of *Rosa*
Sing because of *Billy*
Run because *Jesse*
Help because of *Harriet*
Preach because of *Sojourner*
Strive because of *Booker*
Lead because of *Thurgood*
Oppose because of *Nelson*
Invent because of *Granville*
Dance because of *Katherine*
Fight because of *Jack*

I *Am!!!* Because they *were*

My Rib

Those *lustrous lips*, those *thunderous hips*, that *beautiful hair* and that *sexy stare* keep me aware of where I came from.

God put *you* here for a *purpose*, because you're one of the main reasons why I've been able to *survive* on earths green surface.

You *love* us despite our *flaws*, and yet some cats got the nerve to call y'all bitch or smeez.

Brothers please THESE! Are *African Queens* who so often deal with so much, and receive credit for so little.

You're *my strength* when the world becomes my *kryptonite*.

I've called on you many times and not once have you turned out the light.

Your *control over me* is so *complex*.

You can make me stand *erect*, or simply feel *regret*.

Your *truest beauty* is shown *without makeup*, and I thank God every day for your *creation*.

I've been given the *opportunity* to *feel* your loves *remarkable sensation*.

I've never seen *perfection*, but I know for a fact that you're the *closest* thing to it.

Your *origination* from a man helps me see why you so easily *understand*....me.

A man can never be 100% if you aren't *present*.

You are *God's Gift* to man.

One that is *seldom appreciated* and at times so hard to understand.

I will *die* for you without hesitation, because you are God's most *wonderful* creation.

YOU ARE MY RIB!

You know you got Me

Whatever you wanna make, I'll be you.

Whenever you wanna rub, I'll feel you.

Wherever you wanna take, I'll go you.

However you wanna place, I'll lay you.

Whatever you wanna feed, I'll eat you.

Whenever you wanna heat, I'll melt you.

Wherever you wanna live, I'll build you.

However you wanna bring, I'll cum you

Whatever you wanna teach, I'll learn you.

Whenever you wanna lift, I'll fly you.

Wherever you wanna jump, I'll wed you.

However you wanna piece, I'll write you

Whatever you wanna give, I'll have you.

Whenever you wanna fill, I'll guest you.

Wherever you wanna stand, I'll reach you

However you wanna trace, I'll sketch you

Whatever you wanna show, I'll see you.

Whenever you wanna sleep, I'll rest you.

Wherever you wanna raise, I'll grow you.

However you wanna love, I'll fall you.

Vision

My eyes asked about you the other day
They wanted to know where you've been
Wanted to know why you weren't in front of them

But I didn't have the heart to tell either one of them
That such time has been spent
And I can't quite say just where you went
Or how you're doing
And who you're with

Its just not with us

No longer will they be able to

Lay themselves upon you
But if the day comes

Where they do find you

They'll look at me

And wish they were blind

To the truth

Of no longer having you

Photos

Photographs found we changed

But love touched us always

Remembering past years together

Smiling

And as the morning winds danced onto the soft flying ocean

Ashes of the sun retire

Awaiting the love of night

Release

Release your energy with mine

Love with your heart

And not with your mind

Think with your soul

And speak with your eyes

Release your energy with mine

During the nights where stars come aligned

Take this one chance

Before we lose time

Live with me now

And Love we'll refine

Release your energy with mine

Poetic Path

I'm still trying to find
'My Voice'
In this world

Not the one of
Men & women

But of words
That construct
Poetic rhythm

What do I
Sound like?
Who am I
In this place?
And where does
My Voice
come from?

This mystery remains

'Cause

I'm still trying to find
'My Voice'
In this world
Of poetic Rhythm
And when I do
Make sure you tune in

My Roses

I would shed my own blood
In order to preserve the lives
In which they live

Give the last breaths
Within my lungs to ensure
Their hearts would never stop

It is my way of life
To protect that which I love
So that nothing in this world
Would scar the petals

Of my 3 precious roses

Side By Side

Silence ran through the halls

Like memories of old times

And with each second that passed

I could hear her soul cry

Her tears screamed WHY!

While her lips just quivered

Her eyes blood red

While her body just shivered

Violence of no sense

Took what was hers

And there were no words I could use

To erase such a hurt

We stood

Side by side

But my hands couldn't reach her

The Depths of My thoughts

In the depths of my thoughts
I find reason to believe
That there will never come a time
For a you and me
There will never be a day
To mark the anniversary of our first kiss
And there will never come a time
For us to sit and reminisce about the days of sheer bliss
On occasion I try to resist these thoughts
But when I look into your eyes
I'm reminded of why
Our hearts can never lie as one
Because to you the yolk that I possess is unequal
And therefore there could never be a union
Between such a people
So you believe
And so I retrieve the reality
That I so desperately wished was a lie
So eager to find some possible chance
For there to be a you and I
But my effort is futile
Even though your heart smiles
Every time it sees my true guile
All the while
You submerge those feelings you have
And the only way for me to keep back tears
Is to quickly joke and laugh
When my real reaction is an emotional crash

9/11

And since that time I've found myself in a love recession
Constantly regretting all my past mistakes

And the signs I ignored that seemed to have sealed my fate
In this here heartache

A voice inside is saying don't stop loving her
But another is saying
That ship has sailed
And my once confident train of optimism
Has since derailed
And now I'm cursed to live in this emotionless jail
Forcefully facing my greatest fear of losing love
And all that it entails

I Hope one day
To find reasoning in all this sadness

But in the meantime
Maybe you can ask your god
To work some of his magic

Blind

As he *kills you* softly with his *words*

You *forget*

That you *deserve better*

See your *self-esteem* should *reign supreme*

Instead it's dead

And your *soul* is *weathered*

You're *blind* to the meaning of *true happiness*

Because you fell in *love*

With a *true thug*

One far from a *poet*

Yet he *shakes-a-speare*

Destroying you with the *heartache*

And *thousand unnatural shocks*

That no *flesh* should *bear*

Sex is the only form of love he knows

Whereas you

Would *sacrifice* your very *life*

For his

Case Closed

Friendship

You have always been a *friend* to me, and our past is the reason we have a history.

Feelings remained although touch was lost, and it would seem as if *fate* had a plan for us, the way our *paths* again crossed.

Unknown feelings begin to surface, while our *friendship* grows and gains new *purpose*.

To you I can express my trials and tribulations, and in return you assure me support and *dedication*.

Being the oldest *friend* to I to date, you know the me most *seldom* see.

In you I find a place of comfort, no lies nor deception, only love and pure *acceptance*.

The feeling of *friendship* which you give me, is one that heals my *soul* completely,

I've prayed to find my one *true friend*, and with you I feel that search will end.

When I die

Will my writings be remembered?

Or will the shrivel up and perish

Like the tree leaves of September

Will the world remember my name?

Or will it take its place next to me

Inside the coffin that I lay

Will my family and friends still celebrate my life?

Or will they forget me once I'm gone

And never think twice

When I die

Give Him a Chance

He's too short
Wait 'til he grows up

He's too fast
Wait 'til he slows up

He's too hot
Wait 'til he cools off

He's too rough
Wait 'til he smoothes off

He's too messy
Wait 'til he cleans up

He's too blind
Wait 'til he sees US

Marissa

Her smile

Outshines the sun

& like a gentle breeze

She gives peace

With innocence in her heart

She is but a baby to this world

She is love

She is a memory

Of childhood times

Ice cream trucks

And Ferris wheel lines

A mirror image of her mother

With a dash of grandma

She is the next generation

Those Little Things

Like that smile
Yes
That smile there

It lives in my mind
The way a lion lives in the wild
Running free
Throughout the plains

It has made its home
In my memory

The way a child
Finds comfort in a mother's womb

That look
Yes
The one you get
When I look deep into your eyes

Its laid right beside me
Since the moment you left
I remember it

That sound
Of your beautiful voice
I can still feel it against my skin
The vibrations of each word
Walking across my arm

That kiss
Yes
From your beautiful lips
I still taste the delicate

Sweetness
On the tip of my tongue

Those moments
Yes
Those very moments

I miss them
And await their return

Love Jones

I wanna fall in love with a poet

A woman whose words have curves

Like the pacific coastline

Who was birthed with a beautiful mind

That happens to dance to the same beat as mine

I imagine myself at a venue

Sitting quietly within the audience

Adoring her performance

And with each word she spits

I feel my intrigue grow enormous

A slave to her every word

I can't help but gaze upon the stage

Admiring her stance and how she shines

Brighter than the sun and all its rays

She has me in a daze

So now I'm thinking of ways

To get her and I face to face

Because I've just fallen in love with a poet

And I want her

To do the same

Beauty

That which you are

Is how beauty is defined

Beauty is in the eye of the beholder

And I shall keep yours in mine

Love Buds

I have tasted
Bitter love
I have tasted
love sweet

I have tasted
Jailed love
I have tasted
love free

I have given
Weak love
I have given
Love strong

I have given
Right love
I have given
Love wrong

I have seen
High love
I have seen
Love low

I have seen
Come love
I have seen
Love go

I have heard
Lie love
I have heard
Love true

I have heard
Real Love
Lies between
Me and you

Little Brown Bird

Did you see that little brown bird
Flapping her wings
Dancing through the clouds
Like an airborne ballerina

So elegant
So graceful
So free

Did you see her glide
Through the sky
Like raindrops in April
Landing on the oak tree
Branches
Just grazing its leaves

So soft
So gentle
So sweet

Did you see that little brown bird
As she flew
From place to place
Leaving her mark
With each chirping sound

So light
So peaceful
So melodic

Did you see that little brown bird
When she flew through the sky
As the bullet pierced her heart
Causing her to die

Did you see that little brown bird
As she took her last breath
Killed by a lovers fist

That had once sworn to protect

Years of Yester

Let the tears of my yesteryears

Stay away from my tomorrows

And may the happiness I pursuit

Wrap firmly around my present

Leaving no room for sorrow to invade my future

Let me look upon the skies and thank the powers that be

For the boy that I once was

And the great man I'll soon be

For the lessons I've once learned

And the wisdom I'll soon teach

Simply Mesmerized

Licked by her lips
Smacked by her hips

Pinched by her hair
Rubbed by her stare

Froze by her toes
Kissed by her nose

Pushed by her thighs
Hugged by her eyes

She got me mesmerized

Trained by her frame
Tamed by her name

Kicked by her breast
Slaved by her sex

Bathed by her zeal
Owned by her feel

Struck by her tongue
Drowned by her rum

She got me mesmerized

Burned by her curves
Thrown by her words

Cloned by her peak
Packed by her cheek

Traced by her nails
Calmed by her trail

Jailed by her lines
Rhymed by her mind

She got me mesmerized

Affected

In my heart

In my mind

In my soul

In my chest

In my face

In my back

In my worst

In my best

In my home

In my love

In my will

In my sleep

In my art

In my pain

In my strength

In my weak

In my rights

In my health

In my nights

In my days

In my words

In my church

In my hate

In my grades

In my walk

In my hands

In my lungs

In my mind

In my eyes

In my lies

In my smile

In my time

In My Mind

I often think of you
On nights I don't sleep

Of the moments
We'd lay Smiling
Face to face

As the sun slowly rose
Its rays would kiss your right cheek
Giving vision to the very spot
I would soon place my lips

The mere meeting of our skins
Would awaken your soul

I often think of you
On nights I don't sleep

Of the times your thigh would peak out
From under the bed sheets
Begging me to return to them
As I would get ready for work

I think of the days

Wishing Well

She said I wish you well

I smiled

Then ran to a wishing well
With a silver coin

And said

I wish that her well wishes
Were filled with the pictures
Of her sweet kisses
Upon my lips

Then I ran back to her
To wish her well

She smiled
Then pulled a silver coin from her pocket

And headed toward

The wishing Well

BlackBerry Beauties

Sometimes I wonder
If my words could woo
Those blackberry beauties
Of poetry

Would Nikki let me hold her hand
If I wrote her
Heart felt stanza?

Would Maya have dinner with me
After hearing the rhyming lines
Of my haiku?

I wonder if Sonia would blush
When I stood beside her
Reciting lines of love
More gentle than a turtle dove
In a prose I wrote

I wonder

Could I get a kiss from Gwendolyn
After spilling the words of my spirit
Into her heart
Like lemonade on a summers day?

If I told Lucille that she
Was the reason for my art
Would she love me?

Sometimes I wonder

If I could make them proud

Stand in front of a crowd
Just so I could shout
Lines that they inspired

Until it sets them on fire
And they all fall for me

They way I fell for them

BlackBerry beauties

Poetic Poison

Sometimes I wish I could sit in a room
Filled with the fumes of black poetry

Let the fumes consume the room inside my lungs

Until it becomes the blood in my vessels

I would then run laps
So my heart could pump blood
Rapidly Through the tracks of my veins

So much that my blood pressure rises
With the inspiration of black poets

And my heart explodes

With a masterpiece

Entrée

I got an appetite that has to be filled

It needs much more than your average meal

And my taste buds won't stop jumpin'

Which tells me they're in the mood for somethin' succulent

I'm hoping you let me take my tongue on a trip around that tasty morsel

You may know it as your torso

Then you can fill me in on how you feeling

And I'll begin feelin on all the things you feel need to be felt

No need to turn back 'cause the cards have been dealt

Besides

I'm already addicted to ya taste

And time is something I do not wish to waste

So let's make haste

Then time is now

And I need you on my plate

Dinner's set for 8

So don't dare be late

'Cause my appetite is tremendous

And you're the main Entrée

BlackBerry Seeds

Blackberries
Those beautiful blackberries

Delicate berries
Black like the night sky berries

Why must we continue to bury
Our beautiful blackberries?

Protect them we must
Nurture them we must
Our blackberries

Our beautiful
Young blackberries

Nightmare Amerikkka

The euro-american dream
Came as a nightmare
From the lands of europe
To the Shores of Alkebulan

Recreation

Have you ever been
Turned into a poem?

Well

Allow me to
Recreate you in verse

Bring you alive
Inside the lines
Of a stanza

Letting each word
Replace a curve
Of
Your essence

And paint your smile
With similes

Allow me to sculpt your body
In rhyme
As I take my time
On the inner workings of your mind

Your thoughts
Your fears
Your Dreams

Let me rebuild the nation of you
Into lines of love

Roses of red
Tulips of white

And replace your elegance
With a Haiku
That looks to Sooth

5-7-5
Or maybe
7-5-7
Whichever captures your benevolence

Allow me to be the author of your rebirth upon a blank
page

Filling the empty spaces with the beauty of your spirit

With each stroke of my pen

There shall be a beginning
But there will not be an end

When I turn you into a

Beautiful Poem

My Darling

I know our love is far from perfect

But in my heart and soul I know it's worth it

With God on our side there's nothing we can't do

And all I ask is to be with you

We've weathered the storm from dusk till dawn

And as time passed on, our love proved strong

The loss of your love means the loss of my life

Therefore I ask the question

My Darling

Will You Be My Wife?

Buddy

My sense of peace has been stolen

And along with the hurt

Regret is what I'm holding

I wish I would have known the future

Maybe I could have changed the course of events

While finally finding the right words to convince

You

To do what was right

But that is a wish that will never be granted

So I am left standing

In silence

Filled with hate

And anger

Becuz I lost you to street violence
When I watched your casket lowered
Into the ground
A chunk of my soul
Followed it down

And Now

I'm nothing like I used to be

The moment I saw your lifeless body

An explosion erupted inside of me

Beginning the start of my emotional

Declining

Since that second day in July

I've felt like I've always been climbing

To a place where I'll see you again

A place where we'll understand one another

Provide respect

And forget

The harsh words once said to one another

Because we would finally know

What it meant

To be brothers

The Missing

Bullet wounds
no bleed

Racist fear
Mixed breed

Lovers heart
No other

Baby's life
No mother

Time spent
No use

Artist work
No muse

Music played
no sound

Moves made
No ground

Trust asked
Lie given

Move meant
No Rhythm

Other Side of Heaven

Clouds shaded the darkest of grey

Rumbles of thunder resound

Exterminating the silence

Where a place of peace

Is replaced by violence

Upon mountain tops

You'll find the hottest of climates

Instant moments

Are felt like timeless

And the clearest of vision

Is met by blindness

In religion

I mean

On the other side of heaven

<u>Thanks</u>

I would like to take this time to acknowledge all those that have helped me get to this point. It has surely been a long time coming and I am so happy to have made it here; finally accomplishing this goal. There have been many people who have supported me, and inspired me along this journey. I want to thank you all for everything that you've done for me. This book is a reflection of my life and my experiences along the way, and how they have sculpted me into the man I've become today.

I want to thank my family, I love you all very much and I am grateful to have you in my corner. I would like to thank everyone who has ever been moved by my poetry, and expressed how much my words have touched you. That is the greatest form of compensation I could ever ask for. You are a prime reason why I have given the most intimate parts of myself within these pages. Thank you to everyone who continuously asked *"when does your book come out"*. Every time I heard those words, I got inspired and I couldn't wait for the day it was complete, so that I could share it all with you.

To my friends, my brothers I thank you all for always having my back. I honestly don't know why I said friends because we are most certainly family. I appreciate all of you and I thank you all for believing in me.

www.ingramcontent.com/pod-product-compliance
Lightning Source LLC
Chambersburg PA
CBHW060424050426
42449CB00009B/2126